To

JoAnn Byrne Todd

her spirit

opened a new reach

ACKNOWLEDGEMENTS

Appreciation for permission to reprint poems indicated is gratefully given to journals in which they first appeared:

All-Time Favorite Poetry for "La Pineta di Migliarino"; *American Scenes* for "Old Trees"; *Ball State University Forum* for "Le Torri"; *Blue Guitar* for "Al Haji Nuhu Takes a Fourth Wife," "Ferrogosto: Viareggio," "Luni," and "Out of Africa"; *Bluegrass Literary Review* for "Matched Set," "Prevarications" and "Thalassa"; *Cardinal Poetry Quarterly* for "Trento"; *Chernozem* for "Bagnio di Viareggio," "Geji Cave," and "War Bride"; *Cyclo*Flame* for "Hardscrabble Homestead"; *The Family Treasury of Great Poems* for "You always hated watches"; *Haiku Highlights* for "Background" and "Pride's Corner"; *Hyacinth & Biscuits* for "Il Vecchio"; *Illinois Quarterly* for "Tartiglia"; *Jean's Journal of Poetry* for "Return to Center — I"; *The Laurel Review* for "In the Gallery"; *The Linguistic Muse* for "Tiger Cat"; *Lock Haven Review* for "Tzin-Tzun-Tzan"; *Morton Fierman Festschrift* for "Tempting Time"; *The New Laurel Review* for "Blackberry Weather," "Elba Unvisited," "Moon Rock," "The Rain in Maine," "Wheel Song," "Why I Never Left Saccarappa," and "You Can't Ignore a Bagpipe"; *New Worlds Unlimited* for "Cambria," "Ceremonial," "I saw you dance...," "State of Maine," and "You beat them all"; *Passage* for "Grand Canyon," "manqué," and "The Land of Michoácan"; *Poetry: Fullerton* for "Antiquing," "Hammock Reading," "Mining the Cellar," and "Musa, Steward, Makes Amends for Losing Our Cat"; *Pulp* for "A boy, a dog...," "Corner Drugstore," "French Club — Kano," "Nostalgia," "Oppressed with Age," "Palm Wine," "San Ceccardo," and "Town Characters"; *Quoin* for "Bibbiena" and "Dark Continent"; *Revista/Review Interamericana* for "Iuatzio Waters"; *Southern Poetry Review* for "Marina di Carrara"; *South Carolina Review* for "Fulani Girl"; *Suntemples* for "Juju" and "Wapa Club"; *The Symbolist* for "Mushrooming"; *Voices International* for "Chiaroscuro" and "Massacciucoli"; *Western Review* for "Lizard Pond"; *World of Poetry* for "Skin Deep."

THE MAGELLAN HEART

by

Donald A. Sears

HARIAN CREATIVE BOOKS

Adirondack-Metroland, Saratoga, New York, 1982

First Printing, May, 1982

Printed in the United States of America at
Hamilton Printing Company (HP) of Rensselaer, New York

Library of Congress Card Catalogue No. 81-85192

ISBN 0-911906-25-8, Case
ISBN 0-911906-23-1, Cloth
ISBN 0-911906-24-X, Paper

HARIAN CREATIVE BOOKS
&
THE WORKSHOP UNDER THE SKY

Mailing Address:
47 Hyde Boulevard
Ballston Spa, New York 12020
SAN 204 0255

BARBA — Cues

A creative act is always a journey, from one state of being to another. If a poet enters academia, becomes a scholar, teacher and an administrator, and then returns to the writing of poetry, where does he come out? THE MAGELLAN HEART, a selection of Don A. Sears distinguished poetry, is one answer.

We need not give these poems a close reading to plumb this observation. But if we do, we learn much about the sea changes a renewed poet experiences. We learn what happens when emotions, heart and mind, transformed by learning, discipline and a sense of duty, are finally "given a local habitation and a name." We understand the nature and shape sensibilities assume once sent to school and then graduated as art. In the process, we also learn how much of ourselves to give and how much to withhold as our contribution to the journey we make with the revived poet. Together, poet and reader, we circumnavigate both old and new waters. In this way we explore and rediscover the very real world of senses, feelings and musings we all inhabit on our way to entering the new waters and lands of THE MAGELLAN HEART.

In doing so, we enter so much more than THE MAGELLAN HEART.

For these poems are personal, personal in a special way that only poetic self-biography can be personal, personal for the poet and personal for the reader. We share the poet's nostalgia of hindviews for we too have never left Saccarappa.

When these poems become so personal they threaten to become excruciating, we are rescued by the poet's seasoned craftmanship. With our Ulysses at the helm we are lured by the siren to sojourn "among the maybes," but only so long as heart can endure and sensibilities stay on course.

Tracing the poet's devotion to his late wife, Orange County Superior Court Judge Oretta Ferri Sears, these hitherto unpublished stanzas explore the impact of her tragic death upon the poet's heart and mind, upon the way he perceives art, love, and life. Proportion and balance, developed craftmanship and matured artistry prevail.

Heart and mind, experience and emotions *are* circumnavigated, yes. The boy pilot has become the captain in full command of his weathered craft. Voyage-wise and matured, he steers us back from lands' ends to familiar shore, home free. This, above all, is the world of THE MAGELLAN HEART. The palpitant past and raw present elevated into the sublime, life has become art.

In summary, these poems are a far-ranging and many-splendored voyage displaying the poet's varied and sophisticated tacks in mood, contents and stanzaic patterns. As such, this volume signals the emergence of a sensitive and compassionate cosmopolitan poet. Harian Creative Books is proud to be dock and lighthouse in this setting forth of THE MAGELLAN HEART.

Harry Barba
Publisher and Executive Editor
May 1, 1982

TABLE OF CONTENTS

THE LURE AND CALL

MAINLAND

among the maybes

THE LURE AND CALL

Thalassa

Your lure and call
Demand the choice:
Commitment to the stormy wrack,
Striking to an unknown deep,
Or to the shore,
Safe sands of dreams.
No other way
Unless to wreck
Sargasso-ward
Dead center drawn—
   Treading water's not enough.

Background

The flaw defines the beauty:
Worm at the root of the tree,
Serpent loose in Eden,
Dragon in Hesperides.

Fragility of creation,
Tranquility too soon gone:
Choose a leaden heaven
To drape your rainbow on.

State of Maine

Northeast the drift—
    In rise of rivers
    Tilt of range
    Strung pearls of lakes
    Flung break of sea
    Against serratic cliffs

To walk pine-tall
    This upland state
    It takes firm foot
    Tense spine, spare frame
    And angular
    Leaning to the right

Pride's Corner

Siding bleaching
Spirit breaking
Grays against a sullen sky
Rust of can
Dust of man
Hopes of house or heart that die
Signposts rot
Crossroads rut
Rainbow dreams blanch and narrow
To monotonous tomorrow

A Boy, A Dog, A Deer

A boy
A dog
A scrub pine path
Opening a glade
Once cranberry bog
An atavistic scent
Earflapping dash
And sudden stop
The liquid brown-eyed stare
Of spaniel facing stag
As a boy, a dog, and a deer
Poise tremblingly in grass
The moment clear and clean
Wild, spontaneous
In a quiet isle of light
Amid surrounding woods
Then
    the boy turns back
A chastened dog at heel
To trace a homeward path
A deer bounds free.

Old Trees

Old trees
Rend beneath the
Storm when saplings bend.

Chiaroscuro

I recall strange lights

    — the phosphor glints on ebon waves
      from moonlight on deserted shore

    — a street-lamp sailing into unknown seas
      behind the tossing leaves
      of wind-wracked tree

    — wing lights of an aeroplane
      winking into sleeping cabin

    — star showers of an August night

    — the cold green thread of fire-flies in the fields

    — the chilling glow of rotting timber
      burning damply in the woods

    — water-purified, the aquarelle of filtered rays
    — the blood-veined sun through
      eyelids toasting on the beach

    — the neon blood of stoplights running
      red on wet tarmac of city street

But more than these I keep a childhood memory

    — of auto headlights swinging up the walls
      and down as each car passes, watching
      from the comfort of my father's lap
      before being carried off to winter's bed

Ceremonial

Crepe-paper poppies stiff on wire stems
We sold in recollection — sorry shams —
Of Flanders reaped and sown before my birth,
Now inches tall, in years just past the fourth,

Proud of the girl-mother with me there
((You let me beat you: I sold more))
Then respite from the blustering wind, a cup
Of chocolate blistering at the lip

And endless ride on trolley tracking home,
The close of yet another childhood game
Before the winter darkness settling low
When fallen paper poppies bleed on snow.

Privates

Our generation knew by six
The bond of war and sex,
The Janus masks, mortality and life.
Our time, the trench between two wars;
Our toys, the rattle of tin gun
Soiling the quiet afternoon.

A careless step, a land-mine's burst
And casualty, I sprawl on earth
Wounded as always in one place.
Quick, semaphore the front-line nurse:
Blunt fingers fumble at my fly,
Peruse a shrapnel-shattered thigh.

Jake Barnes, I lie insensate
In the hands of Lady Brett
Till ordered back — the push is on.
A sniper's shot sings out reverse
Of roles, and doctor now I delve
For bullet lodged in hairless cleft.

Induction came to us this young
And basic training was not long.

Hardscrabble Homestead

Retained in the retina of the mind
An image:
             low white farm with ell and barn;
Two hackmatacks, black fingers to the sky;
Orchard green with walnut, pear and apple —
Bittersweet, Wilding, Winesap, Snow, and Crab,
Baldwin, Russet, Macintosh — To name them
Is to taste the individual tang,
To smell again the warmth of field and pine,
To hear cicadas drone above the rushing
Brook, be once again a boy waist-deep
In August's second crop of hay, mindless
In a timeless never-ending day.

Memory's image clouds:
                the orchard fades
To one gnarled tree drowning in a sea of weed;
A pile of slowly mouldering wood that once
Was barn; a cellar hole that once was home.
Tar-papered now at ground line like a tent,
A squatter's subterranean start,
Both start and finish of projected house.
Dessication of the spirit echoes
In this desecration of the land,
A farmland four long generations rich,
Capital scanted, squandered in a day.
Taint of devil's-paint-brush in the hay.

Why I Never Left Saccarappa

Some places you think you want out of
But you never know —
Take Saccarappa, place of falls:
Even the Abenaki, naming it,
Set their nets, fished their fill
And basketed the catch to higher ground;
Nor too unhappy when the saw mill reared
A town between their forest and the sea,
They moved down country to the Kennebec
And disappeared.

Meanwhile the town shaped lumber for the ships
Of Falmouth, Portland now, and drudging wagons
Plied the dozen miles down stream
And broken horses dreamed escape:
 Old horse! old horse! what brought you here?
 "From Sacarap to Portland pier
 I've carted board this many year;
 Till, killed by blows and sore abuse,
 They salted me down for sailors' use.
 The sailors they do me despise;
 They turn me over and damn my eyes:
 Cut off my meat, and scrape my bones,
 And pitch me over to Davy Jones."

Not only horses take the downward slide:
I just can't wait to leave this burg, she sighed,
But

Why I Never Left Saccarappa (Continued)

Mister Austin, since I've been in Boston
I've had my fill of pleasure and I've had my fill of pain,
My brain's been in a constant whirl
And I'll be much the wiser girl
When I go back to Saccarappa, Maine.

MORAL: Some places be good for horses, Indians, and daughters
        Who river-like can't wait to reach oblivion's waters.

NOTES: The popular Portland sea ditty is quoted from Richard H. Dana, Jr., *Two Years Before the Mast* where "stone" appears for the alternate word "board" in line 3. Sacarap or Saccarappa is the early name of present Westbrook.

The second ditty appeared anonymously in 1897.

Mushrooming

wood soil	earth smell
leaf loam	mushroom
tan top	elf cap
rain left	wold gift
slant light	maculate
brush hid	cock's head
hard sought	ground fruit
dim lair	musk spore
mold home	mushroom

Lizard Pond

I'd known the lake for more years
Than I had rememberance of;
For me, it had been always there
And always had been called by that strange name,
Lizard Pond.

Summer days I used to poke about its brink,
Letting the water and the cloud drift help me think
The kind of thoughts a boy will uncover
If he yields his boyishness
To nature and lets the two of them discover,
For him, what he needs to know. I always
Thought that sometime in some such daze
I'd find out too in a sudden guess
Why they called it Lizard Pond.

Certainly there were no lizards on its shore:
Not even tadpoles hid among its shallows,
Nor newts or efts or snails amid its mallows:
As boy I could have found them—if no more—
But there were none.
I solved the other mysteries
Of where the inlet slid its way among the trees
And where the turtles came to sun,
But not that central one
Of where the name came from.
Once I thought I heard the secret

Lizard Pond (Continued)

In the almost human hum
Of a dragonfly
As it droned by,
But I listened too hard and its voice went dumb.

The other day I returned that way
Looking out with other eyes—
Another self, you would almost say.
Seven thousand feet above the land my plane,
A monster dragonfly,
Skimmed the air with a drowsy sound
Of early days when solitary men
Traced paths and mapped the ground,
Naming each part as they strode by.
I roused to see what could be seen
And saw my pond all lizard in its shape,
Head and tail and feet spread round
A silver body set in green.

Without this chance to catch it
From a plane, I never would have found
The lizard shape that made its name so fit.
My childhood mystery was changed
To a deeper and more human kind,
Of an unimaginable man who'd ranged
The woods and who had somehow striven
To its banks to sense how outlined
By the shores a lizard slept.
What mystic insight could have given
Him the name of Lizard Pond?
Others later must have felt derision
(Earthbound as they were)
At this his cloud-born vision
Perpetuated in a name upon the land
As permanent as the water and the sand.

The Rain In Maine

Down-East the coastal people
See these mackerel clouds
(That open and close like sea-anemones
Tickled by a granuled tide)
As predicators of a storm to come.
They tell me with a certain pride
> *Open and shet,*
> *Sign of wet.*
I smile. I know a tired saying when I hear it,
Salty superstition, I don't fear it.
And yet I smell the change of air,
The rising breeze, a darkening everywhere:
The heavens open, as they say.
The rains have come —
> O weeping willow! what a wet
> A drowning drench of a drink
> A dousing dose that plops
> Entire, no drip of drops,
> Cascade of water
> Without stop or let —
Pounded I feel as stripped
While stripes of rain wash down
My head, my back, my chest.
Sky and sea and land are one great rill
I wish for gills
And fishlike gasp for very life.
They say I should have guessed
That heaven weeps torrential tears
When the devil whips his wife.

Nostalgia Poems

A few short forty years ago
When work was hard and living, easy
Our world seemed endlessly the same
Yesterday, today, tomorrow
And yet we woke to find it gone—
Confused, we query with regret:
   Do we, since it was good, now rue it;
   Or was it only good because we knew it?

I HAMMOCK READING

   Back then in the rearward tract of time
   Bees threaded the clover into strings of whirr,
   Sun speckled the chiaroscuro grass,
   Breeze stirred the shadows, whirled the thought
   Of a hammock reader on a summer's day,
   Leisured immersion in the world of Dumas,
   Walter Scott and Maddox Ford,
   Conrad, Cooper, Thomas Wolfe
   Writers who gave the joy of amplitude
   And knew it takes a well-packed book
   To ride a hammock into odyssey.

II CORNER DRUGSTORE

In the vee of a flat-iron building
The corner drugstore was cool and slightly dark
Its quiet stirred at midday by the lazing
Broad-blade fans revolving overhead.
In doorway light the magazines
And pulps cascaded down the wall
Liberty, Galaxie, Bluebook, Post,
True and — forbidden for a boy — the old
Police Gazette and *Spicey Western*
("Through her diaphanous gown Tex
saw the swells of flesh...")
Then angling back along one total side,
The soda fountain — mahogany with gleams
Of spigots, squirts, and porcelain knobs
Labelling the pumps for root beer, Moxie,
Hay's 5-Fruit, and sarsaparilla;
The row of mushroom stools, the spidery
Wire chairs and tables each with silver
Kiosk of Daisy straw. There we ate
Frappés, sodas, sundaes, and floats
Or nibbled papery waffle cones.
Across the back, the pharmacy,
Between the tall amphorae, red and blue,
Gave glimpses on an inner room
Of alchemist's retorts, pill presses, scales
While ranged below, the packaged potions offered
Panaceas: Sloan's Lineament, Bay Rum,
Lydia Pinkham's, Camphorated Oil, Pink Pills,
Absorbine Jr., Nujol, Kickapoo

Medicine, Father John's, and Castor Oil.
Angling back, the circuit led
To boxed cigars, tobacco, pipes and
Luckies, Players, Camels, and Old Gold
For lighting at the cupped gas flame
Flaring on a post; to herbal candies
(Canada mints in paper sacks and
a wooden barrel of hore-hound drops),
A Kodak center and a countertop
Rotating stand of picture postcards
Already fading into history—
A magic store of treats and treasures
Ruled by the Druggist clad in white,
Van Dyked and nodding like an owl,
Wizard of a world to browse and dream in
And to my childhood eyes, ancient,
Changeless and unchanging.
                    Today well-lighted
Walgrens, Thrifties, Rexalls offer more
And less. The corner drugstore is no more.

III MINING THE CELLAR

Today we mine the cellar,
Threading down the tilting stairs;
Bent to spare a scalping from the beams
We enter tunnelled dark and cool
Where boxes, bins and stalls await
A prizing eye.
             Open with care
These relics of the past, handle with love
These cherished things, outworn but yet
Too good to throw away: oil lamps
And pickle crocks, lanterns and clocks,
A broken banjo and some thunder jugs,
A Larkin desk, some Turkey rugs,
A rusting scale, a diking spade and books—
Books spilling everywhere: Peterson's
And Godey's ladies books, hymnals amid
Sheet music when Johnny came marching home,
A Practical Surveyor, Ouida and Henty,
Ryder Haggard, Dickens, Riley, Wister,
Burroughs and Zane Grey intermixed
With family photographs; dim dead faces
Brighten to reflect great-grandchild's eyes
As then and now connect and meld.
Who delves in this ancestral vault
Of memories stumbles onto mother lode:
These veins of shelves and nooks were packed
By human pressures and with golden ore.

IV TOWN CHARACTERS

Just yesterday
The streets were garish with town characters:
Boyfaced Buffalo Bill weathering to age
In western uniform and flowing mane,
Selling papers in the windy square;
Mumbling Minnie cursing all young men
As revenants of the one who jilted her;
The ferret-eyed gate keeper popping out
When the B & M came tearing through;
And Hooker Mitchell (he'd lost that hand
One drunken fall beneath the trolley car)
Telling strangers in the town
He'd left it to a shark
Off Java chasing whales;
Ne'er-do-wells and drop-outs,
The fragile-minded and the barren seeds,
Each had a place, afforded
By a town secure and unafraid
Of those who limped behind a different drum
And dared to live a saving dream.
Transients too were given hospitality,
The bums arriving in the robin spring,
Ready for a hand-out at the kitchen door
Or lick of work if work they must;
Our sidewalks blossomed with their handiwork,
Hieroglyphs of cross and circle marking
Here, beware a vicious dog (the lady too's a bitch),
Or here's good meat and drink.
But then one day the stream dried up
The bums were gone, the characters had disappeared:
Colorless aridity sweeps the canyoned streets
Where faces wear a bland urbanity.

V WHEEL SONGS

Today I long for rumble of wheels,
Rattle of wagons over cobbled streets,
And clop of hoofs in counterpoint:
      —the clink of bottles in the morning dark
      —the smell of new-baked bread delivered fresh
      —the di-syllabic cry of Ra-ags, Ra-ags
            from the cart of bearded Shylock,
            black-coated, reining slack the oldest bag
            of bones that ever passed for horse
      —the tinkling, jangling bells of tinsmith,
            ("Any pots, old pans to mend?")
            of scissor grinder and umbrella man
      —the barnyard fragrance of the vegetable man
            sprawled on a wagon doubling from his farm
And summer afternoons, the best and last
      —the ice wagon, frozen joy of children
            hitching rides and snitching chips of ice
            to tie and slurp through handkerchiefs
            (they strain the dirt and sawdust out)
            the ice-scales swinging at the back
            the dripping trail along the ground
            the lethal pick and giant tongs
            and great wet apron, shiny rubber black
            worn backwards like a batman's cape
            by iceman slinging up his blocks of ice.

For centuries the cavalcade of wagons
Filled our streets and days, but now are gone;
Bereft, I live in wagon loneliness.

Prevarications

Being but indifferent honest
I suppose I've lied since then
But not deliberately,
That was the first.
She knew and I knew
But neither spoke:
Between us tensed the lie
Because — Not me, I cried,
The one to spoil
What she had little of,
A something to be prized.
Round-eyed I'd gazed up at a sky
Flowering with the beauty
Of a golden dahlia, rising sunlike
Rayed and full, her pride;
I stretched my four-foot height
To touch and smell,
Hearing, before I felt, the snap,
Its glory hanging limp.
Today, a hind-sight hypocrite,
I'd twist my error into gesture—
I picked it as your present.

Blackberry Weather

Last of summer gifts and best,
The blackberries drape each road
And woodland path, their red
Burned purple-black at last
And swollen with the dews of dawn.
You'll find the biggest near the sea,
Thumb-thick, inch-long, tugged down
Among the marsh-grass spikes the way
All ripened things are drawn to earth.
But don't neglect the upland yield,
The meadow midgets tart and wild,
Nipped by the first sharp tang of north
That punctuates the still soft air,
The haze of heat, the hum of bees.

These quench a thirst of more
Than summer drought; they lure
With yet another proferred branch
And you're shoulder-deep in a patch
Of blackberries, and it's August, for
Maine to me is always August
And the call and taste of one more
Blackberry before the frost of fall.

Massacciucoli

Stop here, here where you feel the roadway swing
And dip around the hill, leaving the lake
For a moment out of sight, to bring
Us to the center of the town — if center
Can be counted by its one cafe and widening
Of the road. Just here where the hill is set
With antique hand-hewn stone, Etruscan wall
That arcs along the drop-off to the wet
Of marsh.
        The place demands a slowing down,
A searching for some relics of a past
That lingers in the rhythm both of soil
And human kind whose toil and lives outlast
A changing pace, whose ways keep tenor with
The gentle seasons of a lake-shore land,
Whose ploughshares grate on broken plinth and shaft,
Whose vineyards strive to cover monuments and
Tombs, whose daily steps are steeped in dust
Of more than last year's death.
                Stop here and take
The footpath through the break in wall. Here just
Above the marsh, like some old builder's sketch,
Appear the outlines of a Roman house,
Earth mounds drawn in mould, draped in vine of vetch,
Rooms rooted in the ground: atrium, bath,
Cubiculum are here. And still the fading
Shape of black-tiled sea-horse swims in milky
Marble chips before the door, evading
Still the monstrous jaws.
            Stop here and pause.

Luni

Between the sea and alps of Luni
Grapes are swelling on the vine
While breezes cool the sun of Luni
To liquid sunshine, Luni wine.

In the fields strange men are digging
To expose the Roman stone
Of pharos, amphitheatre, and forum,
An archeological zone.
For growing grapes for *vino*,
The finest alluvial soil;
The cost of this one perfection,
Slow centuries of toil.
But no more over Luni
Will the vineleaves spread,
For the living are expropriated
And the soil must yield instead
An antiquary's collection —
Stone-crop of the dead.

Sunning on a stone-flagged terrace,
Built of marble from the past,
An ageless farmer sips his *rosso*,
Warms a tired body in the last
Slant rays of afternoon;
But the fading sun of Luni
Cannot thaw a soul congealed

Luni (Continued)

Nor smooth a face, brown and furrowed
As his vineyard field.
For soon, too soon,
With each excavated yield,
Through man and land, a blight:
Until every field lies
Ruined. Luni dies
As Luna once more comes to light.

No more beneath the alps of Luni
Are grapes swelling on the vine
While breezes cool the sun of Luni
To liquid sunshine, Luni wine.

Marina Di Carrara

Marmoreal Carrara: Under Mediterranean sun
The marble peaks, snow-white
Between the Mary blue of sky
And *mare* blue of sea,
Endure — *pietra dura,*
Sheen and glaze of terra
Cotta, della Robbia scene

Il Vecchio

Flagstones, dimpled by five hundred suns,
Polished by five hundred snows,
Ripple, waver in a golden dance,
Flow about an old man's knees,
Wash upward with an evening peace,
Touch the walnut face with bronze,
Suspend the coming night in day's repose.

Above this living relic of the past,
Dying rays pick out the Ferri arms,
Ancestral homestead, roots that last
As such things do in twisted-tendril hand
Of one old man, il Vecchio's.

You speak: and from a sea of memories
He stirs to meet your New World spouse:

  Che fa! Padroni come, padroni go,
  Some stranger than the last — that one
  The widow brought — Barone of Rome
  She says: in fact, I say, Tedesco—
  This too will pass: so much is done.
  So few remain; the chapel has
  So many, vaulted to the dome,
  The old one too — escomunicato
  For seizing on il Papa's land.
  Arrives the new la Ferri husband,
  In California found, she says,
  Un altro padrone in the line!

  Il padrone Americano! Benvenuto!
  Vieni, taste and test the new red wine.

Tartiglia

Stand here on this grassy terrace
Above the Etruscan wall,
The stone house of Tartiglia
Beside you, and one view will seem to call.

Straight there is the tower of Poppi
Where the Guidi lived and reigned,
This land and farmhouse theirs
And all in sight and more.
For the hauteur of the Guidi
Assuredly disdained
To view from a turret window
A horizon not wholly theirs;
Farm and farmer, crop and store,
All was Guidi. Below
That pinnacle of hill still lies
What is left of Castello di Romena,
Theirs to abandon centuries ago.
That curve of silver? The Arno,
Florence bound, a languid way,
Up here, pure Guidi waters;
For you're in the Casentino
Where the Guidi long held sway
Till at last they ran to daughters

Tartiglia (Continued)

And they wed their lands away
To Bourbons, Alberti, Ferri;
An abandoned land today
With its ancient farms deserted,
The ancient life destroyed.
On its hill the tower of Poppi
Stands tenantless and void,
A ghost staring empty-eyed
At a factory's perverted
Chimney that mocks at Poppi's pride

Stand here on this grassy terrace
Above the Etruscan wall,
Where the stone house of Tartiglia
Yet looks to its Poppi, towering over all.

Trento

No cardinal flame
And less of Mary's blue
Warms the granite pass
The wind-etched rock;
Austere
Severe
The legates huddle
White and gray and black
Sunless shadows—
On this rock....

Elba Unvisited

Elba became visible this morning and stayed till noon.
— Cronica di Viareggio

Loom of Elba from the strand —
Rare to see, to feel the call
Of battered sides of savage rock.
To sense the exile silence
Reaching here and now
Hushing with such lack of sound
I hesitate, lest a breath
Will tear the tissue of this air,
A tautened web of white and blue,
Woven in warp and woof of sea.

I thought to seek that quietude
To climb today the lookout height
But in this fragile gap of time
Elba retreating in the mist
Demands a severing sea between:
I shall not yet approach so near.

Bagnio Di Viareggio

That second umbrellone from the sea
Is mine, was last year and the year before—
Neither native Tuscan who has learned
The grace to live in little space, speaking
Close in friendly *confiance*, respecting
As taboo your miniscule of beach,
Nor Briton burning under *sol leone*,
Lion sun, with glacial Northern stare
Aloof, reserved, would dare approach, much less
Encroach upon my sand, my folding chair;
Tedesco then — of course! the Hun of old
Is boldly poaching on my *Lebensraum*—
Gehen Sie aus, Va t'en and Go away!
This riviera is no playground for the rude,
This crowd no pack of lemmings swarming home;
Each one's unique, observing courtesy:
He'll take his own but never cross the line.
That second umbrellone there is mine!

Ferragosto: Viareggio

No birds fly and no dogs walk;
Even the eternal Tuscan
Voices cease to talk
As off the littoral steals the haze,
Humid heat of August days.
Seaward a single sail drops down
And
        All along the burning sand
The naked flesh burns brown.

La Pineta di Migliarino

A richly living slice of woods
Between the autostrada and the Leghorn train,
These pines have held umbrella hoods
Against the sea-fed sun and rain
Almost it seems the ages since
The last of Rome marched out against the Hun
Along Aurelian Way, their glints
Of steel still seen through all this green
And brown preserved by ducal right,
A park, memorial to their days,
Where we can wander in the filtered light
Down foot-carved paths of hushing haze
That lure us deeper than mere footsteps measure,
Hiatus of the now, the shadow's keeper,
This fusion of the past with present pleasure.

You Can't Ignore A Bagpipe

Picture me a twilight warm and fair,
Awning stirring in the sea-sent air
As cafe-calm of evening's quiet talk
Pervades the promenade where lovers walk
And weave a bright-tomorrow atmosphere.
A flawless fabric rudely torn by shrill
Cacophony, a scrape of sound as if
A cat drew claws across the slate of night,
The first high squirl of pipers from the hill,
Three mountain herders coming to the sea.
Commotion tearing quietude, the clowns
Advance, in lead a lanky grape-stake shape,
All wrist and ankle, followed by a pair
Of bandy legs below rotundity
And rabbit eyes of flutist in the rear.
The bagpipes squeal and squawk like sacks of bees
Confined; they set hysteria humming
For an adage warned us of their coming:
> Rain will follow sunshine
> As A will follow B
> When pipers from Abruzzi
> Travel to the sea.
Go away, Abruzzi pipers, here's lire for your pains,
Don't cloud our sunshine, take your sheep your rains.
Those bladders full of fury can only bring
A deluge, for, like Shylock, our gods
Discharge their water when the bagpipes sing.

Tiger Cat

looks at the sea:

Blue like skim milk in a flat zinc pan,
Mutterer like Old Tom prowling his yard,
You've never known my purrfection of an after-dinner nap,
My dozing in the sun, one eye ajar.
Your white-furred tails switch every minute,
Your ceaseless growl has nothing feline in it.

greets the fishing fleet:

Water laps the pile beneath my feet
Down the shadows flow the laden boats
Sliding with the sun to harbor home
Now on the breeze nose-twitching scent—
Twilight, time for dockside acrobatics
My chance to share these piscine aromatics.

meets twelve Italian Grayhounds:

A movement on the sand like seabirds,
Crouch now, observe the flock approach
They skirt the water's edge on piper's legs,
Four feet, bending at the knee like pacers
Not birds, they sport two kinds of tail
The male wear them curling front, erect,
The female, modest, curve them to the earth,

33

Tiger Cat (Continued)

The grace of each creates a coursing pack,
A flowing feline motion, yet they lack
The je-ne-sais-quois of a cat's divinity,
Boisterousness betrays their canininity.

        outrages Nonna:

Pretend asleep, atop the cabinet
She doesn't see the peeping slit of green
A chicken breast, her supper, simmers
Inebriating scent, yet wait
She sets it on a dish to cool
One feral pounce, uninterrupted streak
Across the floor
The open door
The bonus pleasure of La Nonna's shriek.

Le Torri

Shattered Bacchus in the shrubs,
Shuttered windows, vacant tubs
Where no longer flowers fade:
Above, a sandstone balustrade
Scales as softly into dust
As silent spiders drape
The gateway's rust—

A land reverting to the old,
An upland barren — rocky, cold,
Empty of all human shape
But one too ancient-delicate
For holding in or out the land:
Her head, a snowy weight,
Has earthward curved the back:
Feet stumble, scuffle sand
That stains like mold the black
Of dress—
        A life too late
Along a lifeless track
Where all ahead, behind is dearth,
Lost amid the dying glooms
Of outworn life on worn out earth,
Hollow with Etruscan tombs.

San Ceccardo

Here it began:
On its own hill
With vista of Cararra quarries—
Scars like snow-drifts
In the clefts of cliff—
A villa sheltered under pine and palm
Above the wishbone road,
Its double stairway
Swinging round the niche
Where peeling statue shales
To marble dust
And cactus in the cracks
Bristles like the lone last keeper
Of Baratta pride.
A prickly wisp of woman
Stubborn-proud against the garden
Tangling, tumbling to the town below,
Against decay within, wealth fled,
As calcifying age descends
In chalky splendor,
Final settlement of time—
Here it began
Here ends.

Bibbiena

Also the Cardinal—
Once retired here,
Locked a grated door
Upon the tortuous street.
Climbed the cupped-out marble stair,
And traced the parquet floor
To a frescoed room.
There whispers of his slippered feet
Seemed reminiscences of dialogues,
Sharp and diamond-bright
As a duchess' little finger ring;
And mythic figures on the wall,
Mere shadows of that company
Who echoed solely in his silent thought
As vanities renounced
>   For solitude well bought.

So too your father—
Came back here at last.
Behind a blank and crumbling wall,
Like some worn image of the past
He moved within his garden
To the rhythm of a rose,
Only lifting now and then
His eyes to La Verna's height
Another refuge from the world,
>   Cloud-draped symbol of repose.

So shall we too—
Ascend one final time
That hill-top town,
Ancient refuge from the plain,
Withdraw one final time
And wall our lives around,
The world to lose,
>   All love and self to gain.

Ponte a Poppi

Deep in the Casentino
Centuries linger on
Slow wear of rock
Age told in stock
Of olive tree
Ring by twisted ring

On hillsides sempiternal
Tamed by suspended farms
A foot-carved maze
Of roads whose ways
Run backward
Cusp by curving cusp

Time stopped at Pont' a Poppi
A bridge's doubled span
Millennial
Perennial
Casentino
Stillness of the hub

The Land of Michoácan

Here the countryside is never wild
As we know wilderness of moss-hung trees
Or crashing cataracts or red-baked desert rock.
Such wildernesses we have known
Are never tamed like these
That breathe a gentle air more mild
Than doves. Never here the shock—
In spite of wooded slope and conic hill
(Volcanoes of the not long past)—
Of wind across the vacant spaces, blown
By devil trumpets high and shrill,
Of darkness closing down with terror,
Of emptiness of landscape void of man,
Of tangled paths that foster error
And leave the wanderer aghast,
Bewildered whether all his skill can
Ever get him home, fearing perhaps
He'll have to live with all outdoors,
Slide backwards through all human time and lapse
To brute that creeps upon all fours.
      But not so here where man and nature blend
And all the soil is drenched in human toil.
The loneliest mountain path that seems to end
In outer nowhere opens at a bend
On planted fields and straw-thatched roof:

The Land of Michoácan (Continued)

A half a dozen sunny boys rush out
Welcoming with a universal boyish shout,
While from the door the girls give shyer proof
In their open smiles, of settled days and ways.
Here children grow amidst the growing things,
And all man's furthest wanderings
Return him to humanity:
A shepherd driving home his flock,
A patriarch dreaming underneath a tree,
A guardian dog collecting from the rock
His long-necked goats, or farmer turning up the earth
Along the time-etched furrows of his land.
Here is the blending, here in Michoácan,
Of seasons of earth and seasons of man,
Cycles of birth and death,
and birth.

Tarascan Names

Adventure touched this people long ago
When their agrarian life (so slow
It drifted with the almost unseen clouds
Across the sun-filled sky) met the shrouds
Of priests and armor of the mounted knights,
Went down before acquisitive Cortez
In futile and before-determined fights:
Opposing ways of deed and thought as
Antipodal as life and death, their death—
The rainbow capes of feathers quite outfaced
By suits of metal wrenched from underground,
Deep caverns where the evil gods abound.
Suits of iron, robes of black encased
The pallid men whose skin, fish-belly white
Loosed upon a solar world the dark of night.
For all they touched was tinged with dark and death;
The very god they worshipped, they had slain;
They ruled with terror, torture, fear, and pain.
How could a people comprehend, whose wealth
Was told in children and in ears of maize?
How understand the love of gold, the craze
That valued dross above both growth and health?
Down, down the old ways went before the new,
But over centuries the conquered grew
In quiet strength of not forgotten ways
Until today they keep again the sun—

Tarascan Names (Continued)

Bright days when man and nature are at one.
Alive again the smiling eyes and laughter, for
The high adventure of conquistador
Is happily forgotten like the haze
Of dawn when noon has dried the fields,
Except in some deep corner there may hide
A patch of fog not yet erased by day.

Yet something lingers from the past,
A past forgotten saving when it yields
Some old romantic names once borne in pride
And now conferred, acclimatized at last,
Upon the living crop of boys and girls
That rise to meet us all along the way—
At the injured point this growth of pearls—
Such prevailing beauty we have met
In names: Alfonso, monarch of his hill;
And merchant Marco Polo, wandering still;
Retransplanted here from far-off Spain
Ferdinando, Isabella reign
Again in childhood game; and one more yet,
The little fellow toddling round the bend,
That's Del Fino, the living end.

Tzin-Tzun-Tzan

Between the adobe walls of baked red earth,
The mud and grass strewn street tipped
Upward and became a path that slipped
Around the pools of last night's rain and stopped—
Or seemed to stop—at stone-hewn cross,
Guardian arms to bar the way.
But patient feet, here turned aside, had worn—
Mere shadow on the ledge—
A track that twisted hard to meet
Again the path which climbed beyond,
Now strongly etched along the edge
Of corn fields ripening in the August sun,
While always on the height
The pyramids of Tzin-Tzun-Tzan soared bright
Into the brilliant sky. The path ran
Ever upward over terraced ground
As with each step the careful foot found
Broken flint, obsidian chip, or shard
Of shattered pot, the rubble trace
Of old Tarascan race.
Too gentle to withstand the march of sword and cross
These ancients early disappeared, burying deep
Their tombs and temples under dirt and dross
So long ago tall trees grow there;
And flowers, filling every monumental step, toss
Flaming heads of yellow, pink, and red—

Tzin-Tzun-Tzan (Continued)

The natural decoration of the dead.
Yet in the sudden smile of a native boy,
The old race flashes into life,
Its unity of field and sky and man
Revivified in youthful joy.
And once again the pagan,
Bright and clear and fair,
Bursts godlike from behind a cloud,
Sundering the blood-black Christian shroud.

Iuatzio Waters

Across the milky waters a cathedral soars above
    old trees,
Too far removed to touch the lake with even shadows of
    its spires,
And overhead no drifting cloud disturbs the clear
    expanse of blue,
While floating in between a world of water and a world
    of sky
Our boat is wakeless as it glides in to the shaggy shore.
A hush of more than here and now informs the air,
             And everywhere
             Is still with more
             Than natural peace;
             The hush conspires
             To hold and woo
             Us. Now to die
Would be as passing gentle as the slowest downward slip
    of sleep,
Or entrance into watery chambers where the purest
    dream will keep
Its cool, green-lighted life beyond all whirling worlds of
    human death.
Or like my love as fragile-strong and precious as an
    indrawn breath.

Bauchi Bird

Follow the downward track
That twists through fields of corn,
Skirts round the barren rock
And cuts across the swale and climbs;
Approach in silence and in solitude
What seems a block
Of stone perched high
To catch the earliest streak of morn,
A megalith when nearer viewed,
Hewn in long-forgotten times
To shape of gray-hued hawk,
Rooted in soil,
Restive for the sky;
Watch how you walk,
Lest haste or self despoil
The awe still due the Bauchi bird,
Silent and sacred as the Word,
Like man, from birth
Soil-bound to earth,
Awaiting still to fly.

Dark Continent

We used to call this sub-Saharan land
A Continent of the Dark, perhaps since
Dark-skinned peoples living here amid the sand
And rock had yet received no lightning glints
Of Jesus' or Mohammed's Word of God,
Or since the darkness of our ignorance
Left a universal blank in all our maps.
But whether by design or happenstance—
A plot of mission-zealot priests, perhaps—
The epithet is less than apt, plain odd
To those of us who come to know the eye
Of pitiless and ever blazing sun
That burns away the dross, the inbred lie
Of Europe's civilization.

Under skies as blue as vast,
Our strength is backward cast
Upon ourselves. No prop
Outside the lonely center of the self
Can stop
Our going wrong if wrong we be
For whiskey, women, sloth, or drugs.
Dwarfed in this clear light,
Man's bigness shrinks to that of bugs,
Unless refined and rarified,
The flesh dissolved and scarified
By day, with no escape by night,
When soft and sensate
Under stars so bright we see
To read the fate
And fortune in our hand,
And learn to love—and hate—
The omnipresence of this vivid land.

French Club — Kano

Blue, green, red, the lights wink on,
Festooning trees that can't obscure
The equatorial stars,
Bright in the African night.

The self-same colors echo
In the Sepoy uniform
Of six-foot-two Fulani
Before the inviting door.

The ice has been delivered,
The Star Beer properly chilled,
The discotheque is waiting
In the *libraire* to begin.

The members slowly gather
In pairs, in family groups,
With here and there a single —
Nowhere else on earth to go.

For pilots in from Bruxelles,
Or daughters of the Levant
Ripening so far from home —
A lark, dancing in the dark.

For wives of British exiles,
For construction engineers,
The week revolves about this
Hub of an African club.

Phantasmagoric figures
Forget about *domani*
As under colored lights they
Swell a Breughel scene of hell.

Wapa Club

Dark shapes lurk by the break of wall
Shadows tunnel the entrance hall
Nostrils snuff the privy scent
Take offense at the sweet of sweat
Relax, release, relent
Too late to return, repent
Highlife drumbeats fret
A vibrato center
Lave with fire
A secret wire
Enter, enter

Tabled cells rank the wall
Open-air roof and a concrete floor
Blood-dyed bulbs obscure the gloom
Shape and shadow jostle the room
Drug-smell smothers
Evil hovers
Hidden knife and surface grin
You come, hah, you come in
Dwarf-man, big-man here
Big-man, big no more
Dwarf-man, big-man here

See naught, seek naught
Reach the door
White-man come to Wapa
Club no more

Geji Cave

In fastnesses no guide
Will enter, the Geji still abide,
Precarious on a hilltop
Where corn and tillage stop.

On a sheltered outcrop
Of a shelving cliff
Are painted gods, totemic;
Cattle — frozen in rock;
Birds — arrested in flight;
Fish — suspended in height;
Ochre shades on gray as if
Animate-inanimate were blended,
Man himself appended
As an afterthought.

Clacking lip-plugs signal
In inhuman speech
Naked Geji women;
Demanding hands outreach
For "Dashee, gimme dashee,"
Toll from those they shun.
They want "Shilling-
Shilling, one for one."
But the words clack chilling
On that mountain sill
To anyone who wanders
Too far on Bauchi hill.

Juju

We cross the dust-draped fields above the stream,
A sandy yellow gash this season,
To the rock-heap rising through the moated air
In sun-bleached gray of high noon-day.
Boulders hugely strewn beyond all reason,
Piled and jumbled by a god at play
Who sportively tossed his granite toys aloft
And balanced one or two cigar-shaped forms
On high: on closer view like fish they seem
Swimming in the fetid haze, sky-borne
In the stream of air, precarious
Guardians of a lair.
            Perilous
To enter here, for even at broad noon
A reek of fear like damp from underground
Breathes on us signs from the fissures that we pass
In clambering up the faint-etched path
To an opening at the utmost top,
O'ershadowed, darkened by the swimming fish,
A grassy flat, a circle ringed with rock.
Central, like a jewel in a mount
Of straw, a strangely blackened altar-stone,
A plaited switch of grass, a human knuckle bone.
Withholding from the lips the rising query
One learns to treat the unknown with respect,
Make no remark on what has been remarked
But sight across the altar stone and through
The break of natural walls — due east, where moon
Will rise as it has risen on a throng
Expectant in the night. Now none too soon,
Turn back and seek the safety of the guide
Around whose neck there flashes into view
An agate fish suspended from a thong.

Musa, Steward, Makes Amends
For Losing Our Cat

I have surprise for you;
I got them all, wham-bam.
Just look in every bedroom,
    See many puss, madam.

You say you like small cat,
The way I like sweet yam;
I spend the day in hunting
    Many puss, madam.

At first they run like lizard,
They fight me like wild ram,
Don't want to stay in quarters,
    These many puss, madam.

I grab them by the neck fur,
I put in room and slam
The door. They no get out.
    So, many puss, madam.

There's one in every bedroom,
The biggest one I cram
In yours and doctor's bathroom.
    Many puss, madam.

Yellow, tawny, gray ones,
One like gooseberry jam,
All are mad like cobra,
    Many puss, madam.

I get all puss in Kano,
Even Miss Moody's Tam.
You like surprise of Musa?
    Too many puss, goddam!

Al Haji Nuhu Takes A Fourth Wife

Wife Number One grows cranky,
Her ills with age increase;
While Number Two refuses
To give me any peace.
My former favorite, Three,
Cares more for women's chatter
Than for her husband's solace:
So much seems the matter
That I sleep much too little
And eat too much by far;
If I weren't an Al Haji
I'd go to the Christian bar
And drown my boredom there
In drinking strong Gold Label,
But I am a big Al Haji
Unable to drink, but able
To marry me another wife.
I follow my father's wisdom,
Who said, "When tired of life,
There is no tonic for boredom
Better than this I give:
A fresh young wife refreshes
And recalls you how to live."
So enough of brawling quarters;
I go to Lagos town.
I'll get me a Fourth to marry—
And then I'll settle down.

Palm Wine

Seven black crones
Seven charred vats
Seething in a row
Cackle of age
Crackle of branch
Fires burning low
Acrid smoke
Simmering sap
Bubbles bursting slow
Slack mouth
Bent back
Flat breast
Leg of slat
Dust and pithless
Dessication
Old woman's occupation

Fulani Girl

Romantic scene from a 1930 film
Rescreened against exotic setting,
A dusky Sheba tempting Solomon,
Salome offering to remove a veil—
   Cocoa queen, straight as palm,
  Agate-smooth between the guinea corn
   And conical mud huts,
  Knowing motion of presented cigarette:
  "Master, light me cigarette?"

Out Of Africa

Heavy hearts above the desert
Seething brains above the plain
A hundred odd we sit assigned
Ticketed, noted, checked, O.K.'d
Relaxed and prosperous, all resigned
We watch a past slip by and fade
Ties slip and sever
Good-byes are forever
Here the only dangers
Are a letting go
Of all that desert-land below
Where friends are future strangers.

MAINLAND

Grand Canyon

Out of the canyon curving downward zone by zone
The wildborn wind rose sighing in a steady drone,
Its first faint pressure on the cheek
So slight that we might speak
Of it as a cat's-paw brushing by
(Except that cat's-paws play and go away
And come again — and this was here to stay).
The pressure grew, perceived at last
Only if we stopped and thought, when time had passed.
"Yes," you said, "It's stronger now.
The trouble is we cannot stop to think
When time is blowing off the brink."

Still louder surged the wildborn sound:
We leaned against its force so hard
That had it stopped we would have jarred
Against the red-rock ground.

I felt it calling from the depths,
Fought hard, with reason, to implant my steps
In the solid rock of canyon rim,
But lost the fight and lept
From rock to rock to reach your side.

A mountain goat, you named me,
Laughing above the mounting tide,
Recalling with your eyes our recent night
Havened in one another's arms
Against the harms outside.

We stood against the wind-voice (now a roar),
Blown clean of self, blown free of mind.
The roar a message we might almost understand,
We waited hand in hand

Grand Canyon (Continued)

For something more,
Patient and sure
That it would come.

It came.

You saw it first — far down the canyon deep,
Fantastic, massive, a wind-etched shape
Of Indian god — the Hopi Thunderbird,
The voice of wilderness they sometimes heard
Speaking to their wilderness of human soul,
As now it spoke to two on the edge
Of something stronger and more fragile than the ledge.
Like birth and death it engulfed us whole
In darkening wings and sounding air
Till we were one with the one down there.

What had we seen?
What had
It said?
What did it mean
To two alone
In a world of stone?
We could not say,
We could not run away;
Strengthless we stayed pinned
To its brute strength
Swept clean, through all our length,
Two changing children of the wind.

After our night
It took a god to grip like fate
And swoop us to this primal height —
Solitary, man and mate.

Gleanings From The Yácata

Five hundred feet below, the water gleamed
Clear blue, so purified by height
Of all the reedy mud and clay
That show its surface milky gray
To those who only see the nearer sight.
Yet viewed from here its azure seemed
A perfect match for azure sky,
Responding, light and shade, to drift of cloud;
Patzcuaro waters, from the yacáta, allowed
Five hundred years of time to fade and die.

Closer — squeezed between the farms and shore—
The village slept in 'dobe red and tan
A dream-held landscape as of yore
Persisting over Christian ban
In rhythmic life of ancient ways.

Now closer, on the upper slopes there strays
A girl who walks the fresh-ploughed field
In silence to and fro along each row
With eyes cast down and back bent low
To scan the ground for sudden yield
Of shard or chip or broken vase,
Recollection of a vanished race.
At home so far from home, Etruscan
Travelling up and down Tarascan
Hills in stance as old and wild
As any gleaner, as young as any child.

In The Gallery

Past the winged statue by the pool
And through the tunnelled cool of marble busts
Of Greco-Roman greats staring stonily
At the woman and child who sit with aching feet
Beneath Bernini's flying head of Louis Quatorze,
Past such memento mori of the men
Of wars long gone, I wander room by room
Each richer than the last in oils of North
Italian Renaissance.
                Sated then with wealth
Of color and the stealth of wit which lit
The dim religious figures, I am drawn
By a whispered promise of a special treat,
While here and there the patrician stare of a proud
Firenze noble, in calm yet startled scorn,
Looks out at the foreign sight of my fleeting form.

In the ninth room, shunning the clutch of viewers
Before the small madonna of famed Raphael,
Amid ancestral glut of portraiture
I stop, and turn, and find you, in the eyes—
In the gold-flecked dark-brown eyes, ghost-haunted—
Of Di Credi's portrait of himself before
He'd met Savonarola and had learned
To burn the pagan in his soul as he
Had burned the pagan pictures of his youth.
Five hundred years of time dissolve as your eyes

In The Gallery (Continued)

Gaze from old Lorenzo's youthful face.
All other antique eyes had looked out blank
As stone, insouciant in pride, but here
The golden brown looks inward to a soul
Severe and sensitive.

                       The eyes were right—
Pure you — but all the rest was out of skew
To one who knew perfection of your face;
Here the cheek too full, the jaw too long,
And a mouth not worthy of a second glance,
But oh, the eyes—translucent, ambergris.

Pygmalion

The artist smoothes the slow cool curve of back,
Cupping his palm to round the rise of cheek—
Lets the hand linger longingly,
In love with the perfect fit of flesh and stone—
(He knows how few things fit in this rack
Of time — this wreck of mine and thine.)
Rapt in his timeless world he thinks he stands alone;
The moment lengthens like the easy creep
Of dusk on summer nights, extends, distends
As eyes go blind and the body glows.
The pores drink in the seeming musk
Of marble — the Carrara warms to sudden rose,
A woman throbs beneath his touch, forsakes
The frozen stone and once in love awakes.

War Bride

Violence, always the background.
Impinging like the subtle sound-
Track of a television show—
Known and heard, not listened to,
Perhaps enhancing the quiet round
Of daily life:

      Child of war-torn
Florence, in expectation born
To life of pride and castle-calm,
Wrapped by servant care from harm
Of daily strife,

       You grew with death,
Rubble dust polluting every breath,
Sewage seeping through the water main,
And on the walls the hidden stain
Of dark decay.

      And so you grew,
Mortality defining all you knew,
Till with the courage of your race,
You turned a fresh and eager face
Toward dawning day;

       Or so the dream
Of life beyond the sea would seem
To one so young. Yet even here
The world was old, the old ways sere
And nearly dead.

       Then love — almost
Too late to raise and rouse the ghost
Of other ways — like rain to earth,
To you brought neither death nor dearth
But life instead,

And you, whose breeding was majestic,
Find joy is thoroughly domestic.

Return To Center — I

I knew you as an object — nice to view
    Or as a thought to be explored.
So held myself at guard from contact with the you
    I scarcely felt the woman who might be adored.

For she was buried deep — a dream I once had had
    And locked away in a mental room
I built to keep the bits of life both good and bad
    That didn't fit. There like attic heirloom

Overlooked and yet not wholly out of mind
    Your image dwelt — waiting for a key to turn,
A light to pierce the gloom with slantwise shine
    In which the outer you would move like fern

In forest glen yearning across space
    To its ponded self. Thus when we met
A light broke through like a sudden grace,
    Far off a door key turned to let
        You enter—
    My dream returned to center.

Cambria

Today we do the beach
Two rock-hounds coursing
(Between the cliffs and rattling tide)
A fog and wind scoured coast,
Each searching for the gift
Of moonstone, agate, jade,
Of trilobite or mollusc fossilized.
　　Eyes dazzle in the watered light
And stoned I wander from your side
Obliterate in spray and sand.
Time holds its breath
And all is changing changelessness
As shadows shrink from length of morn
To dot of noon; a warmth invades,
　　And then a waft of woman scent
From — is it steaming kelp? —
Draws me to your waiting hand:
Instead of wave-washed gem
Myself I find, in you,
Lodestone, woman, wife.

Moon Rock

These boulders sprinkled on the shore
Are charactered in petroglyphs by time,
Aeon-etched to individuality.
Each slow lapideous life
Delapidates from macro-stone to micro-sand
In millennial rhythm
Only seeming sedentary.

Beneath the flashing lights of breaking tide
They wash and wait and
Sometimes ask a questing hand
To lift and take them home
While others less adventuresome abide
In place, maturing to the quiet
Artistry of carving sea,
Abrasive wind and tensing sun.

By day a reticence of secret life
Withdraws within itself
And then, reality appears
The motion of the ebb and flow
Around a scattering of stone-dead rocks.
But when the moon succeeds,
The rocks commence their dance,
The lapidary lines retreat, advance
Like sea-hens wading in and out
Until no longer can one know
                    whether
The waters dance and the stones are still
                    or
The stones dance and the waters are still
Respondent each to moontide will.

Antiquing
For Oretta On Our Tenth

As rich mosaic covers somber wood
Your rarities smooth out my former years,
Allay my fears
Inlay with good
What was of strength,
And bury underneath your beauty
Cracks and flaws of former duty;
Across what seems a momentary span,
The patient days advance the artistry,
A decade's length,
That welds a woman
And her man
To ageless art
That has been building all along,
Precious, delicate, yet strong.

manqué

somewhere still

the lonely child

fragile small
rides a cold stone
dreams deferred
and yet despite
delicate of limb
as inward soft
when watered by
sprout deep in dark
to choke today
how then can
compensate
revive the child
and extirpate

yet iron willed
lion into
by promises unkept
she grew in beauty
as outward strong
where seeds of hurt
the tear unwept
curl and coil
in yesterday
daily caring
or heal-all love
to joy of now

the tendrilled past

Matched Set
To Oretta On Our Twentieth

I scored, you scored, who scored
That day, a double decade past
When passion from a winter sky
Swept over, through us, left us wrapped
In love—

      — the game of life
Was yet to play, though then began
The orchestration of two themes,
Each one unique, but neither deep
Nor rich without the other's
Counterpoint —

      — the scoring
Moved in time, a doubles match,
Till midway in the set, Time Out;
And there upon the board abide
Two perfect scores —

      — all tied.

among the maybes

In memory of Oretta Ferri Sears
(1928-1980)

And did you know
(in your somewhy heart)
That you would go away?
So long ago
You promised
(and never failed to keep your word)
To fill me with yourself,
All other memories overlaid
        (Finding out I once
        had spent a weekend
        at Point Sur,
        You'd rush me there
        to love beyond
        love-making)
Until
Saturate with you
I have no other,
Known no other
Every inner where is you.

The hand still curves
To fit the feel of flesh,
Memory in the pulse
Still holds it open
To the mirrored mold,
So often felt,
The long, so longed-for touch
That arced us into timelessness,
All pasts collapsing into now
And all tomorrows squandered lavishly.

With you my hands were full.

You tricked me when you slipped away
And left the clock's escapement
Clicking out each time-balked day:
You who always played so fair
Locked me into ticking time, where
Reaching out, the hand encloses chilling air.

Our love began skin-deep
My palm along your cheek,
The later lower cupping
Of the swell of breast
Rising to meet me like
The rising of your groin
All ways the joining
Pore to pore
Unity from two
Who made each other
— Made for each other —
Miniscule matching flesh to flesh
Flesh in flesh, a perfect fit
In a world unfit.

Then gone
Divided by the grassy turf

Last night our daughter
Woman grown, older than the you I met,
Crying, sought the comfort of my arms
And for a moment on her cheek a hand
Felt pore to pore the magic grow,
Incipient incest, if you will
But beauty in forbidden knowledge —
Such matching does exist and did exist.

No deeper love than love skin-deep,
Depth of flesh not elsewise plummetted:
Who had it once will walk
The world skin-hungry, ever after

Deepest thoughts we spoke in silence
Thrilling through the blood
But other times we talked the stars away
And woke to talk again.
In resonance almost masculine,
Your voice, vibrant, subtle, low,
Crept into my ear, neglected orifice
Dimmed by dinning of the world
Defenseless portal breached
Before I knew, my inner being
Reached and probed by timbre
Of your voice.
     Still now in the night
When full moon shines me into wakefulness
I feel you speak of love we had.

Why do I keep on writing love songs?
Now that your voice is stilled?
Flinging poems into the void of air
Another shout
That we were here,
We felt, we loved,
We gave the world
Its more than due
When we it was that counted
Not the palms and plaudits
Though these came,
Extraneous, enjoyed
Because we shared
In secret secret strength—
And so in habit now
Again I fling
The fragile words
Against the falling night.
We had the best the world
Could give, each in each
And it was never near enough.

From centuries your line
Had — when I met you —
Run its course
Down to four women
One of whom I had to love:
    Nonna, white in black
            a trotting self-contained,
            contented wraith with
            skin of watered silk—
    Mamina, little mama
            never grown
            beyond the pampered
            girl whose limit of compassion's
            "How could you do this to me?"
    Daughter, beautiful of body
            seeking any way the father
            who rejected
            as he'd pedestaled
            her babyhood—
    And you, surrounded
            leeched upon
            sole keeper of responsibility
    The wonder's not you ended soon
    But that you lasted it at all.

★　★　★　★　★

How could husband-lover fend that scheme?
What room for the dream we dreamed:
            You sought escape for us—
            Our flight to Africa
            An interlude too brief
They found us out
Their empty need
Draining drop by drop
What we had nurtured, grown:
            If cliffs wear down in laving sea
            And granite scars in loving wind
Can flesh, can blood
Endure?

Day by night
You pulled the fences down
I thoroughly had built
And used the salvaged pieces
To surround the two of us made one
With paling to close in
Our secret world.

When you slipped through,
You tore the paling down:
Peeled to the core
I'm naked, flayed
And shall I, how,
Build walls again?

        These bricks, moss-covered now
        And warped by roots
        You laid in carved-out niche
        Of 'dobe earth
        Disdaining sand
        (Who builds upon the sand...)
        Paving a future path
        Too brief
            Bare toes embrace the ice-cold brick
            Once warmed by your domestic hand.

You beat them all
The other women of my life
The growing sixteen years with mother
A year or two of mistresses
And sixteen more with her who gave
Me children, adults now, and yours—
All others bested by our twenty years
You won

But where do I find victory?

When others pull their blinds
Nesting within
I walk my solitude

The play of minds
The shift of thoughts
Turned and tried
Upon each other—
Intimacy more than flesh
As two brains mesh
Cogs of cogitation:
    My books, you were in them all.

A special spirit in your birth
No source for which in parents can be found:
The petty, ever-talking self of mother
The solitary sodden pride of father
In you welded opposites
Public proud and private shy
Caring and not caring
Spending without sparing.

At our best we did outrageous things
Hurling them at time:

    The two of us connected, chatting and laughing
      with your husband through the phone
    Your call to me on New Year's eve, stirring
      my suburban party with disruptive love
    Telling Bobby K in velvet-collared coat
      how he'd forgotten Alabama
    Your dancing naked on my bed
    3 a.m. and waking hungry to demand Room Service
      telling some Italian chef to build a
      lovers' salad for us two
    The drink you threw in Teddy's face, some years
      before he learned to freeze it on the bench
    That night we took the Justices to the Gaslight
      Club along with two stray hookers I just asked to join
    Or skinny dipping at the Country Club by stars
      in Palm Springs summer heat
    Your honesty, direct—How many women in your life?—
      when first we rose for air from weekend
      snowbound while our spouses raged...
Love ran strong and life seemed long
    As we laughed the nights
    And worked the days away,
    While others carved a monumental life
    We tossed it like a ball
    And played it as a game
    For keeps.

Public eyes perceive:
        Middle-aged
Hair boyish short and tinged with gray
Snapping questions from the bench
Wearing dignity with grace
Certain of respect
She sits as judge of the appellate court

My eye reflects:
        Mediterranean sky
The flowing sun-flecked mane of hair
The racing down the beach
Alive, I'm alive
Don't saddle me

They didn't fence you in.

Among the maybes
Of voluted time
Our ancestors met and bred
Descendents spreading
To two continents.

Orbited together,
Recognition in the blood
Of self to other, self in other,
Bonded us, steel to steel
(the Ferri of your name)
Molecular cohesion
—not the casual joining
of two human solitudes
such as the world accepts,
good marriages—
With us, familial welding
Yet distinctly two of body
Beautifully female/male
As if twins from a single egg
Were yoked again, yang and yin;
We could not feel where ended one or one began.
Not just in rich tempestuous tide
Of passion but in daily breathing,
Mirrored self of one from two—
Inbred similitude.

So many times
Cradling you, my sleeping child,
Within my arms
I stared into the dark
Outstared a face
Of mocking evil
Drawing near,
By concentration of the will
Forcing back what
Came impinging, seeking you.

I held you, had you, so
So long ago in otherwhere
And waited O so long till found,
Fierce then to protect
Through each dark night...

O not again the endless walk
Alone...

One night of calm I fell asleep
The mocking force
Stole close and stole you
From my keep
Now old, I start once more
The endless walk

Of course there was a something impious
In our love,
Adoration of incarnate flesh.
Knowing (but never having known,
Never to know) better,
We took it as your gift, God,
We took it for eternity.

For me, she came before You;
For her, I was an all:
I worshipped at a woman's shrine
For she was cleft for me;
She bowed to me her living David
And so she cleaved to me.

Earth replaced celestial yearnings,
We chose terrestrial joy;
Helpless to change, not willing to,
We knew we tempted time.
It happened thus and we embraced
What might have been Your grace—
And was it also, God, Your envious hand
That reached us to destroy?

One courage is the way
You faced real danger —
Surrounded by Geji natives
Or with Thompson pointing
Through the window of your car
You never changed your manner
Never honed your tongue
To superficial smoothness,
Acknowledgement of fear.

The greater courage was to face
Interminable tracking of each day,
Mind assaulted by the lip-plug clacking
Not of Geji but of friend
Day by day erosion
Of the inner self
And night by night in the dark time
Before a never-coming dawn
To hear the mocking question
To what end?
                    To what end

Before we could begin our life,
With the knotted past undone,
And reach the lovers' goal
Of simply one on one,

We had to span the continent,
Complete what was begun
In a snowbound weekend
Of simply one on one.

Three years of heaven and hell,
The victory hard won
Though all we ever wanted
Was simply one on one.

When we'd put ourselves together
Others sought us on the run
Intrusion we resented
Upon our one on one.

Everybody wants in the act,
As Durante said in fun;
There is no room for others
When you're simply one on one.

I saw you dance with Don Carlos
Bourbon y Bourbon, your cousin,
In black-trained gown of Spanish lace,
Mantilla and diamonds in your hair.

I saw you also dancing in the tide
Of Cambria's wild shore,
Now overalled and sneakered,
In a cast-off shirt of mine,
From your tresses sun-flecks
Flashing in the air.

Beach bum or princess, this is written
By one who loved you, contrast-smitten:
All life you treated with a flair
And death you ran to meet, still debonaire.

Heat unrelieved at midnight
Flight to beach, and moon, and stars,
Where, straight out, you walked
Into the moon-pathed waves
Following a call of the sea,
The dark

Later, warmed in my serape,
We loved against despair,
And looking upward through your hair
I wished upon a falling star.

Still later, you would laugh
About your tumble in the surf
"I had to get cooled off
and nearly drowned."
I let you laugh the lie
The secret in my keeping
Of a moon-drunk path
A midnight shore
And dark

It wasn't that
You loved me
And thus let me
Be myself —
With you
There were no bars
To be let down
For you were open
Warm and free

In your love
I swam an element
That thawed me
To an inner ease—
No censor screened
My barefoot word,
Unbuttoned act:
The thinking was to say,
The feeling was to do,
A single flow
No must or ought or have to
Your loving drew me out
In freedom
Of to be

The Santa Ana turns the air to dust
And as I lean to walk
The body recollects: our start
Poised upon Grand Canyon rim,
The wind-roar from the depths
That swept us free of dead encumbrances;
The interlude of Kano
Where the Hamatan cooled our days
And warmed our blood;
And now
         the nightly howling of the wind
         Around the hollow eaves

It had to be, I thought at first,
Another of your famous stunts,
Those unexpected shocking acts
Of deed or speech you did so well:
Telling the head of the CIA
To go and fuck himself.

This time you really did it, though,
And I can't heal the wound, no way
To smooth the surface with a gloss;
Nor can we share the afterglow
Of just another stunt.

No retraction, no way back at all
When you have laid upon the world
Your last and lasting Fuck You All.

I curse the dying foetus in your womb
            the man who grew it there
                  and, locked in Catholic pride, refused
                  the therapy, abortion
I curse your night-long days of screaming pain
                  that pushed you into death and back,
            your ruined gut —
My childless mate, who now
Will treasure our lives' treasures?
To whose keeping may I trust
The memories, the trinkets, home and ground
You trod?
            No child of ours, though
We rode Desire
Farther than is granted most.
Your stop came before your time
And now a solitary transient
Rides to the ending of the line.

Here by the Pacific shore
You never could be pacified—
On edge of more
Than continental shelf
You swung between extremes:
America, adopted by the will
Italy, land of childlike dreams

And so the sway
From world to world
A tattered map in halves
You spoke of going home
And yet you clung
To a quiet hub of mate
Till he too
Was an insufficient cause
To stay

One night of calm
Your wild, free spirit
Imperceptibly withdrew
Heart weary
Did it enter
Inward on itself?
Did it find heart's ease
And when the pendulum had stopped
Did you return to center?

It takes the young to understand
I don't want tears and sympathy
But beauty, youth, long hair
They know the ancient wisdom
Of two selfborn needs
Just being, and accepting,
Rolling with the day
To mere enjoy
But most
The sharing the same air
Subtle connecting — mind, exuded woman scent
To match the still young heart, hurt
But stirring.

They never query of my want
But come and give
Their balm of youth.

The years have drawn me outward old
While yet within a spirit flames:
I should have lived to ashen days
Content to sip the sweetened tea
And talk of bowel movements
In the shade
With white-haired ladies, epicene,
And pale old men.

No, rather
Let me go with those
Who woman-wise
Offer cure not care
The captured smell
Of fresh-washed hair
Warm skin
The juices flowing
Sweet and sharp,
Whose eyes, undulled by life,
Brighten the image
Of time-tarnished self.

My days I live with
Daughters of the soul
My young, my women—
The nights, as yet, alone,
For touching would be joy too much
The ending only pain.

This morning
Between the straight tug past the ear
And the rasp along the left jawline
The razor pulled me into wakefulness
As the mirror suddenly unfocussed:
Who was there,
Half-lathered, wavering
From shape to shape?
The well-known self
Or something struggling to emerge?
Bewildered stare
Saw grieving man exchange
With lecherous ape.

For years an inner surety
Described the who I was
Because I loved and won you
Lived you as my wife.
When you took your life
Away, the bonding broke
And from the mirror stares
A formless form, and whether
I'll yet pull my self together
Or blur forever in the steaming glass
I know a man's true outline is
Distinguished in reflections
From his woman's eyes.

Today I started lunching in the cheater's corner,
Taking drives into the countryside of matinées
And joining in the evening misery
Of Happy Hour at the cocktail lounge,
To check the scenery and maybe pick a bit
To decorate my room.
At miniscule tables lost in murk
Knees bump and elbows rub
Talk flows too fast,
The jokes too loud
Here nothing's simpler
Than to take a body home.
But I am twenty years too late
And having lived our mating
I play the ancient game
With futile automatic moves:
No piece is worth the taking
For my queen is gone.

Six months without you
And my first trip back to our retreat:
    Each pine, each room appears a deadly same
But lifeless — boughs hang limp,
Hollowness echoes in the rooms—
And cowarding before my emptiness
I tuck another woman in your bed
As warmth against the silence, dark,
And etching memories.
Our private home
Remains the same
And not the same
For always it existed
Less in space than mind
And so I live a week
In place and give it up,
Keeping only reminiscences
Against the spoil of time
Until I too dissolve—
Till then I share our Cambria den
But have not walked our beach again.

NEW PASSAGE

Jo Poised

Calm in country tweed
Possessed of self
She moved assured
Throughout the social evening.
Suddenly in the pale light of four A.M.
Exiting my door with casserole
And coat in hand,
As I returned from seeing off the last
Departing of the lingering guests,
I saw her, backlighted
By the warmth of open door
Heading lonely into pallid night,
A something tender in the stance,
A hesitation on the edge
Of giving up some final chance.
Dim light revealed the inward self
As no glare could:
I race across the lawn
Fearing to be too late,
I ache to lend support,
To soothe the hurt I felt
In the figure outlined there,
To wrap myself around a small and lovely creature.
There are such moments
When life pauses on the threshold:
We seized it with a knowledge not of mind
And entered through the door together.

Props

I thought it took a lot of props
To hold a shattered column up,
So, hectically enringed my self
With multiple and fragile counterparts.
When you (likewise scaffolded
And guyed with numerous supports)
And I met and centered
On each other's strengths,
The lesser props about us fell away;
I learned what I had always known
That less is more when one—
The fitting one — comes into place.
Straight and firm again I feel
Our bonding hold,
Not complications but simplicity.

Neat Lady

Those who put their lives
In union with the sea
Reflect an elemental grace—
Conrad's shipshape life.
So you, neat lady,
Kept your life
All tidy
Every part in place
Immaculately set.
Did love upset
Or did it simplify?

When it comes to choice
(Societal convolutions
Or inward clarifying)
Better tidy pockets
Of the soul than
Locked-off rooms
Of well-ranged furniture,
My inward tidied,
Newly neat lady
Of my soul.

Laguna by Moonlight

We laugh at foolishness of kings,
Canute ordering the sea to cease,
Midas aureating all he touched,
With touch of love or touch of need.

My sand-gold girl,
Why should we laugh at these,
When touching you,
Eyes dazzle in green haze
And surging blood
Repeats the tug of tide?

Moon refracting from the waves
Patterns white flesh
Phosphorescent in reflected light
As white arms fold
Against a rising wind.
Flesh joins on sand,
Engrottoed safe,
Yet open to the sea and night,
As all the silver world burns gold
And sea and sand and wind and wave
Internalize,
Night pallor warms to gold,
The restlessness at peace.

The Magellan Heart

From rounded warmth of dim-remembered breast—
Child nestled safe—
I grew to go, and left
The homeland coast of Maine,
Out to a world of hot and cold:
The steaming, sweated climb
To reach a Continent's divide;
The frozen shock of dive
Into the liquid snow
Of High Sierra's streams.
Or on to Africa, feet burning
On the sun-parched dust;
Through dark Canadian woods,
Learning to walk on frozen stumps.
Some people spoke of bodily invigoration
Although the heart yet yearned
For the unfound,
                    in between extremes.

The night I found you
(Even though together we may roam)
I slipped into my long-lost
Warmth from half a century's journeying
To find myself
At home
At last.